Team Spirit®

THE TORONTO MAPLE LEAFS

BY

MARK STEWART

Content Consultant
Denis Gibbons
Society for International Hockey Research

NORWOOD HOUSE PRESS
CHICAGO, ILLINOIS

Norwood House Press
P.O. Box 316598
Chicago, Illinois 60631

For information regarding Norwood House Press, please visit our website at:
www.norwoodhousepress.com or call 866-565-2900.

PHOTO CREDITS:
All photos courtesy Getty Images except the following:
McDiarmid/Cartophilium (6, 14, 16, 38, 41 bottom right), Parkhurst (7, 21, 40 top),
Hockey Illustrated (27), Imperial Oil–Turofsky/Hockey Hall of Fame (18, 24),
Topps, Inc. (9, 20, 23, 35 top left & right, 41 left), Author's Collection (17, 34, 37),
Esso (19, 22), Goudey, Inc. (28), O-Pee-Chee, Ltd. (29, 43),
Graphic Artists/Hockey Hall of Fame (31), Hockey Pictorial (36),
The Coca-Cola Co. (40 bottom), York Peanut Butter (41 top right),
Matt Richman (48).
Cover photo: Andy Devlin/Getty Images
Special thanks to Topps, Inc.

Editor: Mike Kennedy
Designer: Ron Jaffe
Project Management: Black Book Partners, LLC.
Research: Joshua Zaffos

LIBRARY OF CONGRESS CATALOGING-IN-PUBLICATION DATA

Stewart, Mark, 1960-
  The Toronto Maple Leafs / by Mark Stewart.
      p. cm.
  Includes bibliographical references and index.
  Summary: "Presents the history and accomplishments of the Toronto Maple Leafs
hockey team. Includes highlights of players, coaches, and awards, quotes, timeline, maps,
glossary and websites"--Provided by publisher.
  ISBN-13: 978-1-59953-338-4 (library edition : alk. paper)
  ISBN-10: 1-59953-338-3 (library edition : alk. paper)
  1. Toronto Maple Leafs (Hockey team)--History--Juvenile literature. I.
Title.
  GV848.T6S74 2009
  796.962'6409713541--dc22
                                              2009022204

COVER PHOTO: The Maple Leafs congratulate each other after a goal during
the 2008–09 season.

Table of Contents

SPORTS WORDS & VOCABULARY WORDS: In this book, you will find many words that are new to you. You may also see familiar words used in new ways. The glossary on page 46 gives the meanings of hockey words, as well as "everyday" words that have special hockey meanings. These words appear in **bold type** throughout the book. The glossary on page 47 gives the meanings of vocabulary words that are not related to hockey. They appear in ***bold italic type*** throughout the book.

Meet the Maple Leafs

The country of Canada covers more than 3 million square miles (7.77 million square kilometers). On the frozen ponds and chilly ice rinks in each of its provinces and territories, young athletes dream of playing **professional** hockey someday. For much of the past *century*, the team they dreamed of playing for was the Toronto Maple Leafs.

The Maple Leafs were the "home team" for English-speaking Canada for many *decades*. Millions of fans followed their games on radio and television. The team rewarded its fans with 13 championships during an amazing span of 60 seasons.

This book tells the story of the Maple Leafs. They may no longer be the only team that Canadian fans cheer for, but no one can deny their popularity. In fact, it is still hard to find a Canadian newspaper that does not cover the Leafs 365 days a year. And millions of kids still dream of pulling on the team's famous blue-and-white uniform.

The Maple Leafs celebrate a goal during a 2008–09 game.

Way Back When

In 1917, a group of Canadian business leaders joined together to form the **National Hockey League (NHL)**. Toronto was one of five cities that got a club. It was owned by the Toronto Arena Company and known as the Toronto Arenas. They won the 1917–18 NHL championship and then beat the Vancouver Millionaires to claim the championship of pro hockey, the **Stanley Cup**. Two years later, the team renamed itself the Saint Patricks. The "St. Pats" won the Stanley Cup again in 1922. The star of that team was Babe Dye. He led the NHL in goals three times.

In 1926–27, Conn Smythe bought the team and renamed it the Maple Leafs. Smythe and assistant coach Frank Selke built the club into a powerhouse. Toronto had two great defensemen, King Clancy and Clarence "Hap" Day. The team's top scorers—Charlie Conacher, Busher Jackson, and Joe Primeau—were nicknamed the "Kid Line." The Maple Leafs won the Stanley Cup in 1932 and reached the **Stanley Cup Finals** five more times during the 1930s.

ABOVE: A souvenir postcard shows Charlie Conacher, a star of Toronto's "Kid Line."
RIGHT: Ted Kennedy, a team captain during the 1940s.

Toronto had an even better club during the following decade. The Maple Leafs won the Stanley Cup in 1942, 1945, and each year from 1947 through 1949. They won it all in 1951, too. Those teams were full of talented players who never quit. Their stars included Babe Pratt, Syl Apps, Gordie Drillon, Turk Broda, Sweeney Schriner, Ted Kennedy, Harry Watson, Gaye Stewart, Billy Taylor, Tod Sloan, Max Bentley, and Bill Barilko. Many of them were voted into the **Hall of Fame**.

The Maple Leafs had several poor seasons during the 1950s, but things began to change when Punch Imlach became the Toronto coach. Johnny Bower was an excellent goalie. Dave Keon, Tim Horton, Frank Mahovlich, Bob Baun, and Carl Brewer *emerged* as stars. George Armstrong gave the team solid leadership. Imlach also added Allan Stanley, Eddie Shack, and Red Kelly in trades.

Toronto reached the Stanley Cup Finals in 1959 and 1960 but lost both times. The Maple Leafs returned to the finals each year from 1962 to 1964 and won the Stanley Cup three times in a row. Imlach never stopped finding new **role players**. By 1966–67, Toronto was an old and aching team. It didn't matter—the Leafs won it all again!

After the success of the 1960s, Toronto fans suffered through 20 years of frustration. The team made unwise trades and lost several good players to the **World Hockey Association (WHA)**. The players that stayed—Darryl Sittler, Lanny McDonald, Tiger Williams, and Paul Henderson—were among the best in the league, but the Leafs still struggled. In the 1980s, the team was led by Borje Salming, Rick Vaive, and Vincent Damphousse.

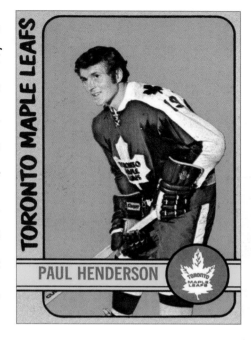

TORONTO MAPLE LEAFS

PAUL HENDERSON

The 1990s were much kinder to the Maple Leafs. Rough and rowdy Wendel Clark was the team captain. Doug Gilmour became a superstar after he joined Toronto in a trade. Later, Mats Sundin developed into the Leafs' top scorer. Goalies Felix Potvin and Curtis Joseph protected the Toronto net, while forward Tie Domi became one of the NHL's top "tough guys."

Toronto reached the **Eastern Conference Finals** three times during the decade. In 1999–00, they won their **division** for the first time in 37 seasons. However, the team could not get back into the Stanley Cup Finals. That challenge would be left to a new group of Leafs.

LEFT: Mats Sundin, the team's all-time leading scorer.
ABOVE: Paul Henderson, a key player for the Leafs during the 1970s.

The Team Today

The Maple Leafs have won championships with very young teams. They have won with **veteran** teams, too. They are at their best, however, when they mix energetic young players, *experienced* stars, and a few "old-timers" who know all the tricks of winning in the NHL.

During the early years of the 21st century, the Maple Leafs tried to rebuild their team this way. They found some talented players, including Alexander Mogilny, Tomas Kaberle, Darcy Tucker, and Bryan McCabe. The Leafs always did well in the **standings**, but they lacked the **team chemistry** needed to advance deep into the **playoffs**.

In 2004–05, the NHL players and owners could not agree on a new business deal. The entire season was cancelled. After that, the Maple Leafs decided to rebuild again. Through **draft choices** and trades, they found the building blocks they needed to return to the team's glory days. Jason Blake, Alexei Ponikarovsky, Matt Stajan, Pavel Kubina, and Vesa Toskala became team leaders. The Leafs and their fans started planning for a new *era* of success.

Tomas Kaberle and Matt Stajan hug John Mitchell after a goal in a 2008–09 game.

Home Ice

From the 1930s through the 1990s, the Maple Leafs played in Maple Leaf Gardens. It was Canada's most famous arena. Fans thought of the building as a "temple" of hockey. Watching a game there was the experience of a lifetime.

Maple Leaf Gardens was a magnificent building—the first hockey rink to have a four-sided clock, escalators, and shatter-proof glass around the ice. The arena was also the site of the first-ever game of the league that would become the **National Basketball Association (NBA)**. Every hockey game at Maple Leaf Gardens was sold out from 1946 until it closed.

The Maple Leafs moved to a new arena in 1999. Maple Leaf Gardens simply did not have enough seats. The new building is located in downtown Toronto and was named after Air Canada, the country's biggest airline. Fans call it the "Hangar."

BY THE NUMBERS

- *The Leafs' arena has 18,819 seats for hockey.*
- *The Maple Leafs only retire numbers worn by great players whose careers were cut short by terrible accidents. Bill Barilko (#5) died in a plane crash. Ace Bailey (#6) was seriously injured on the ice during a game.*

The Maple Leafs take on the Detroit Red Wings in their home arena during the 2007–08 season.

Dressed for Success

The Maple Leafs wear blue-and-white uniforms. But in Toronto's early years as the St. Pats, the team colors were green and white. In its first season as the Maple Leafs, the team also wore green. Today, Toronto's sweater is one of the best known and most popular in all of sports. Thousands of fans buy Maple Leafs jerseys every week.

The maple leaf is the national *symbol* of Canada. The team has worn a leaf *logo* on its uniform since changing its name in 1926. From the 1920s to the 1960s, the leaf was black, green, white or blue, or some combination of these colors. It looked very realistic, with jagged edges. In 1966, the team started using a simpler blue-and-white leaf. The logo players wear today has been the same since the 1970s.

In 2000, the Maple Leafs introduced new uniforms with a more modern look. In addition, Toronto created an alternate logo, but the team also still uses the classic maple leaf design.

A souvenir postcard shows Hap Day in the team's original green uniform and its blue sweater.

UNIFORM BASICS

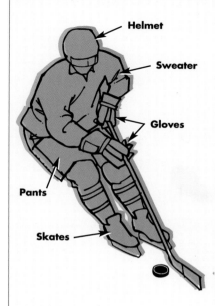

Helmet

Sweater

Gloves

Pants

Skates

The hockey uniform has five important parts:

- Helmet   • Sweater   • Pants
- Gloves   • Skates

Hockey helmets are made of hard plastic with softer padding inside. Some players also wear visors to protect their eyes.

The hockey uniform top is called a sweater. Players wear padding underneath it to protect their shoulders, spine, and ribs. Padded hockey pants, or "breezers," extend from the waist to the knees. Players also wear padding on their knees and shins.

Hockey gloves protect the top of the hand and the wrist. Only a thin layer of leather covers the palm, which helps a player control his stick. A goalie wears two different gloves—one for catching pucks and one for blocking them. Goalies also wear heavy leg pads and a mask. They paint their masks to match their personalities and team colors.

All players wear hockey skates. The blade is curved at each end. The skate "boot" is made from metal, plastic, nylon, and either real or *synthetic* leather. Goalies wear skates that have extra protection on the toe and ankle.

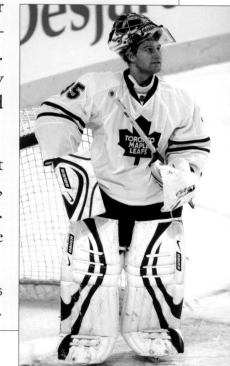

Goalie Vesa Toskala wears Toronto's 2008–09 away uniform.

We Won!

Many people think of 13 as an unlucky number. For fans of the Maple Leafs, it is the luckiest number of all. That is how many times the team has won hockey's greatest prize. The Leafs won the NHL's first league title and then faced the Vancouver Millionaires—the champions of the **Pacific Coast Hockey Association (PCHA)**—for the Stanley Cup. Alf Skinner scored eight goals to lead Toronto to victory in five games.

Toronto returned to the Stanley Cup Finals in 1922 and won again. Now known as the St. Pats, the team defeated the Millionaires again. Babe Dye scored two game-winning goals to help Toronto beat Vancouver in five games. Dye netted nine goals in all, which tied the record for a five-game championship series.

The team renamed itself the Maple Leafs several years later, and then moved into its glorious new home, Maple Leaf Gardens, for the 1931–32 season. Toronto celebrated by defeating the New York Rangers for its third Stanley Cup. The "Kid Line" of Busher Jackson, Charlie Conacher, and Joe Primeau scored eight times.

The Maple Leafs won five Stanley Cups in the 1940s. Their victory in 1942 was one of the most amazing in sports. The Stanley Cup Finals had been expanded to a best-of-seven series. The Leafs lost the

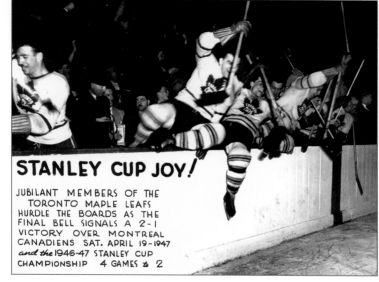

STANLEY CUP JOY!

JUBILANT MEMBERS OF THE TORONTO MAPLE LEAFS HURDLE THE BOARDS AS THE FINAL BELL SIGNALS A 2-1 VICTORY OVER MONTREAL CANADIENS SAT. APRIL 19-1947 *and the* 1946-47 STANLEY CUP CHAMPIONSHIP 4 GAMES *to* 2

first three games to the Detroit Red Wings—and then made an amazing **comeback** by winning the last four games. Little-used Don Metz was one of the heroes for Toronto.

The team's 1945 championship was also amazing. With many NHL players fighting in World War II, the Maple Leafs turned to first-year goalie Frank McCool in a Stanley Cup Finals rematch with the Red Wings. He **shut out** Detroit in the first three games. The Red Wings won the next three. In Game 7, Toronto won 2–1.

In 1946–47, the Maple Leafs were young and energetic, but they lacked experience. That showed in Game 1 of the Stanley Cup Finals when they were blown out by the Montreal Canadiens. Coach Hap Day used the **embarrassing** loss to **motivate** his players. The Maple Leafs won four of the next five games and became the youngest team ever to capture the Stanley Cup.

LEFT: Babe Dye, Toronto's record-tying scorer in the 1922 Stanley Cup Finals.
ABOVE: The celebration begins after the team's 1947 championship.

Toronto won the Stanley Cup again in 1948 and 1949. That team's stars included goalie Turk Broda, defensemen Jimmy Thomson and Gus Mortson, and forwards Sid Smith, Ted Kennedy, and Max Bentley. In 1951, the Leafs won it all again. But their triumph soon turned to tragedy. Defenseman Bill Barilko, whose **overtime** goal won the Stanley Cup for Toronto, was killed in a plane crash over the summer.

Johnny
BOWER

The Maple Leafs of the 1960s were one of hockey's most famous teams. Under coach Punch Imlach, they scratched and clawed for every victory. Toronto raised the Stanley Cup each year from 1962 to 1964, and again in 1967. Goalie Johnny Bower played his best when the team needed him the most, and hardworking players such as Dave Keon, Tim Horton, and Bob Baun never let up for a second. Baun skated the final game of the 1964 Stanley Cup Finals with a broken bone in his foot! Three years later, the Leafs again summoned every ounce of strength against the powerful Montreal Canadiens. Toronto took the Stanley Cup in a *remarkable* six-game victory.

LEFT: Teammates carry Bill Barilko off the ice after his overtime goal that won the 1951 Stanley Cup.
ABOVE: Johnny Bower, one of the leaders for the 1967 champs.

Go-To Guys

To be a true star in the NHL, you need more than a great slapshot. You have to be a "go-to guy"—someone teammates trust to make the winning play when the seconds are ticking away in a big game. Maple Leafs fans have had a lot to cheer about over the years, including these great stars …

THE PIONEERS

BABE DYE   Right Wing

- BORN: MAY 13, 1898 • DIED: JANUARY 2, 1962
- PLAYED FOR TEAM: 1919–20 TO 1925–26 & 1930–31

Babe Dye was a member of the team when it was still an amateur club. He turned professional when Toronto did. Dye was not a swift skater, but he had a hard and accurate shot. He scored 201 goals in 271 games.

ALL-TIME GREATS

KING CLANCY

KING CLANCY   Defenseman

- BORN: FEBRUARY 25, 1903 • DIED: NOVEMBER 8, 1986
- PLAYED FOR TEAM: 1930–31 TO 1936–37

King Clancy had a small body and a huge heart. He could play every position on the ice, but he was at his best on defense. Clancy led the team to the Stanley Cup in just his second season in Toronto.

ABOVE: King Clancy   **RIGHT**: Syl Apps

SYL APPS   Center

- BORN: JANUARY 18, 1915 • DIED: DECEMBER 24, 1998
- PLAYED FOR TEAM: 1936–37 TO 1947–48

Syl Apps was a world-class pole vaulter and a great football player. Toronto fans are glad he chose hockey. During his career, Apps was one of the sport's most admired leaders.

TURK BRODA   Goalie

- BORN: MAY 15, 1914 • DIED: OCTOBER 17, 1972
- PLAYED FOR TEAM: 1936–37 TO 1951–52

Turk Broda led the Maple Leafs to a Stanley Cup before World War II, and then returned from two seasons in the military to win four more. Broda was one of the best **clutch** goalies ever.

TED KENNEDY   Center

- BORN: DECEMBER 12, 1925 • PLAYED FOR TEAM: 1942–43 TO 1954–55 & 1956–57

Ted "Teeder" Kennedy did many things well that often are overlooked, including winning faceoffs. In 1954–55, he won the Hart Trophy as the NHL's top performer despite scoring only 10 goals. Kennedy led the Leafs to five Stanley Cups.

TIM HORTON   Defenseman

- BORN: JANUARY 12, 1930 • DIED: FEBRUARY 21, 1974
- PLAYED FOR TEAM: 1949–50 & 1951–52 TO 1969–70

Tim Horton scared opponents with his incredible strength. When they challenged him, he put them in a powerful bear hug that left them gasping for air. Horton was also famous for keeping his cool at "crunch time." He won four Stanley Cups with the Leafs.

FRANK MAHOVLICH   Left Wing

- BORN: JANUARY 10, 1938   • PLAYED FOR TEAM: 1956–57 TO 1967–68

Frank
MAHOVLICH

Frank Mahovlich was the top scorer on two of Toronto's three championship teams in the early 1960s. "The Big M" netted 48 goals in 1960–61, which stood as a team record for more than 20 years.

JOHNNY BOWER   Goalie

- BORN: NOVEMBER 8, 1924
- PLAYED FOR TEAM: 1958–59 TO 1969–70

Johnny Bower might have been the bravest goalie in the NHL. He played in the age of the slapshot without a mask—and with terrible eyesight! Bower challenged shooters to beat him and wasn't afraid to shove larger opponents out of his way. He was still making great saves for the Maple Leafs well into his 40s.

DAVE KEON   Center

- BORN: MARCH 22, 1940   • PLAYED FOR TEAM: 1960–61 TO 1974–75

Opponents had to keep a close eye on Dave Keon. He was a swift and tricky skater who loved to flash toward the net and catch goalies by surprise. Keon was also an excellent **penalty killer**. He often scored short-handed goals with one of the best backhand shots in the NHL.

ABOVE: Frank Mahovlich
RIGHT: Wendel Clark

DARRYL SITTLER   Center

- BORN: SEPTEMBER 18, 1950 • PLAYED FOR TEAM: 1970–71 TO 1981–82

Darryl Sittler joined the Maple Leafs when they were rebuilding in the 1970s. He was named team captain at 24 years old and soon became Toronto's top scorer. In 1975–76, Sittler finished the season with exactly 100 points (41 goals plus 59 **assists**)—the first Toronto player ever to reach that mark.

WENDEL CLARK   Left Wing

- BORN: OCTOBER 25, 1966
- PLAYED FOR TEAM: 1985–86 TO 1993–94, 1995–96 TO 1997–98, & 1999–00

Toronto fans called Wendel Clark "Captain Crunch." Players who took the ice against him were guaranteed to wake up sore the next day. Clark loved to smash into opponents, but he was also a skilled scorer. He netted at least 30 goals for Toronto four times.

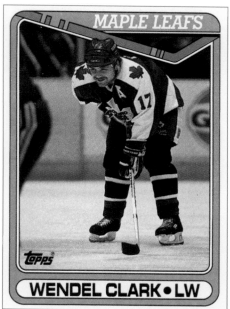

MATS SUNDIN   Center

- BORN: FEBRUARY 13, 1971 • PLAYED FOR TEAM: 1994–95 TO 2007–08

Mats Sundin stood 6′ 5″ but played with the *agility* and quickness of someone much smaller. During his long career with Toronto, he led the team in scoring every season but one. Sundin finished as the club's all-time leader with 420 goals and 987 points.

R.WING   JOE KLUKAY
L.WING   BILL EZINICKI
R.WING   JIM THOMSON
L.WING   HARRY WATSON
R.WING   GARTH BOESCH
CENTRE   GUS MORTSON
R.WING   HOWIE MEEKER
GOAL   VIC LYNN
DEFENCE   BILL BARILKO
L.WING   SID SMITH
CENTRE   BOB DAWES
R.WING   MAX BENTLEY
R.WING   TOD SLOAN
DEFENCE   LES COSTELLO
L.WING   FLEMING MACKELL
GOAL   CAL GARDNER
DEFENCE   FRANK MATHERS
GOAL   BILL JUZDA
                HARRY TAYLOR
GOAL   RAY CERESINO
L.WING   RAY TIMGREN
                TIM DALY, TRAINER

P	W	L	T	FOR	AG	PTS
60	22	25	13	147	161	57

Behind the Bench

As of 2009, no fewer than nine Toronto coaches had been voted into the Hall of Fame. Five made it for their performance on the ice, while four made it for their contributions behind the bench. The most famous Toronto coach was George "Punch" Imlach. He was hired to run the team's business in 1958, and then named himself coach. Imlach had a military background and treated his players like soldiers. They didn't always like him, but they played hard for him. The Maple Leafs reached the Stanley Cup Finals six times under Imlach and won the championship four times.

Hap Day also had a great run of success with the Maple Leafs. As a player, Day combined with King Clancy to form coach Dick Irvin's top defensive duo. Day was captain of the club that won the Stanley Cup in 1932. He returned to coach the team in the 1940s and led Toronto to five more Stanley Cups.

In recent times, the team's most successful coach was Pat Quinn. In 1998–99, his first season in charge, he transformed the Maple Leafs into a fast-skating, high-scoring team that reached the Eastern Conference Finals. When Quinn left Toronto in 2006, he had 657 victories—the fifth most in NHL history.

Punch Imlach poses for a photo with Frank Mahovlich and George Armstrong. Imlach guided the Leafs to four Stanley Cups.

One Great Day

No one doubted that Darryl Sittler was a good player. But for nine months in 1976, he was the best player anyone had ever seen. In the spring, Sittler scored five times in a playoff game. The following fall, he netted a spectacular goal against Czechoslovakia to win the first **Canada Cup** tournament. For most players, that would have been a career's worth of highlights. For Sittler, it was just an "encore" to his greatest performance of all.

On February 7th, 1976, the Toronto center took the ice in Maple Leaf Gardens for a showdown with the Boston Bruins. The Leafs had been playing poorly, and the Bruins were on a roll, so the fans weren't sure what to expect. After the first period, Toronto led 2–1. Sittler had assisted on goals by Lanny McDonald and Ian Turnbull.

In the second period, Sittler scored three goals and assisted on two others. The Maple Leafs led 8–4. Between periods, Toronto's *statistician* told Sittler that he had seven points. The NHL record was eight. Less than a minute into the final period, Sittler netted his fourth goal. Nine minutes later, he scored his fifth goal—and his ninth point

After his amazing performance against the Boston Bruins, Darryl Sittler was front-page news with hockey fans.

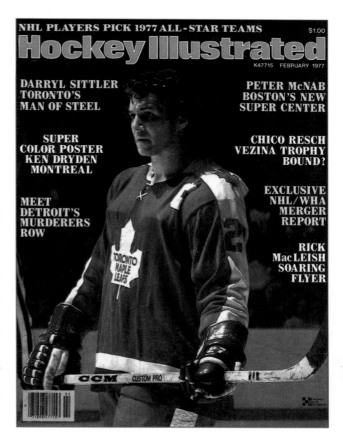

overall. The fans rose to their feet and gave him a long standing **ovation**.

Sittler wasn't finished. With less than four minutes left, he scooped up a puck behind the Boston net and flipped it in front, hoping a teammate would be there. Instead, the puck bounced off a defenseman's leg and past goalie Dave Reece. Sittler had his sixth goal and 10th point of the game. Normally, hockey players raise their arms in victory after scoring. This time Sittler grinned as if to say, "I'm sorry."

"I didn't know why it kept happening," he admits. "It was like one of those days on the golf course where every putt goes in. That night every puck went in the net."

In the Boston locker room, Reece was in a state of shock. The team sent him down to the **minors**, and he never played another NHL game.

Legend Has It

Which Toronto player was responsible for the first All-Star Game?

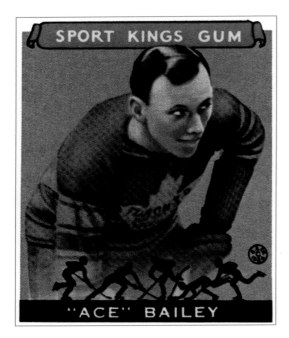

SPORT KINGS GUM

"ACE" BAILEY

LEGEND HAS IT that Ace Bailey was. In a 1933 game against the Boston Bruins, Toronto's Red Horner delivered a hard check on Eddie Shore. Shore was dazed and wanted revenge. He mistook Bailey for Horner and hit him from behind. Bailey fell backward and slammed his head hard on the ice. Fans and players feared for his life. Bailey recovered, but his career was over. NHL players decided to play an **All-Star Game** and give the money from ticket sales to Bailey and his family. During the contest, the Maple Leafs retired his number 6. It was the first time a hockey team retired a jersey. The NHL has been playing the All-Star Game ever since.

ABOVE: Ace Bailey, whose unfortunate injury led to the first All-Star Game.   **RIGHT**: Ian Turnbull, the Maple Leafs' high-scoring defenseman.

Who was Toronto's most "offensive" defenseman?

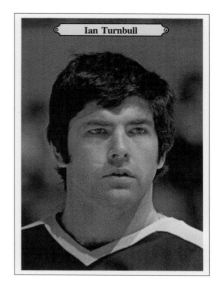

Ian Turnbull

LEGEND HAS IT that Ian Turnbull was. Turnbull played for the Leafs during the 1970s and early 1980s. He appeared in the All-Star Game once for the team. Turnbull had a hard, accurate shot—and it was never better than in a game against the Detroit Red Wings in February of 1977. That night, he took five shots and scored on every one. No other defenseman has ever scored five times in a game.

Did a horse help build Maple Leaf Gardens?

LEGEND HAS IT that one did. To afford Maple Leaf Gardens, Toronto owner Conn Smythe knew that he needed a big star to sell tickets. Smythe decided that King Clancy was his man. He contacted Clancy's team, the Ottawa Senators. They demanded $35,000 for him. Smythe could only afford $20,000, so he went to the racetrack and placed a bet on an unknown horse named Rare Jewel. The longshot won, Smythe made $15,000, and he was able to acquire Clancy. Maple Leaf Gardens later became hockey's most famous arena.

It Really Happened

Athletes and coaches can be a very *superstitious* group. Anything that brings a team confidence—or luck—is worth trying. During the 1970s, many people believed that Egyptian pyramids contained a magical force. They placed small pyramids over their heads or near important items.

During the 1975–76 playoffs, Toronto coach Red Kelly decided to put "Pyramid Power" to the test. Kelly had played for the Leafs in the 1960s and won four Stanley Cups with the team. But now he felt a different type of pressure. Maple Leafs owner Harold Ballard told reporters that his team would whip the powerful Philadelphia Flyers in five games. Kelly had to deliver on that promise.

Earlier in the year, Kelly's sons had traveled to Egypt. They returned with amazing stories of the supernatural power of the pyramids. Kelly hoped they were right. Prior to one of the Maple Leafs' games against Philadelphia, he placed small pyramids under the bench and all over the locker room. Darryl Sittler, the team's top scorer, took notice.

"Red put a pyramid in the dressing room," he recalls. "So I put my sticks underneath it hoping it might help."

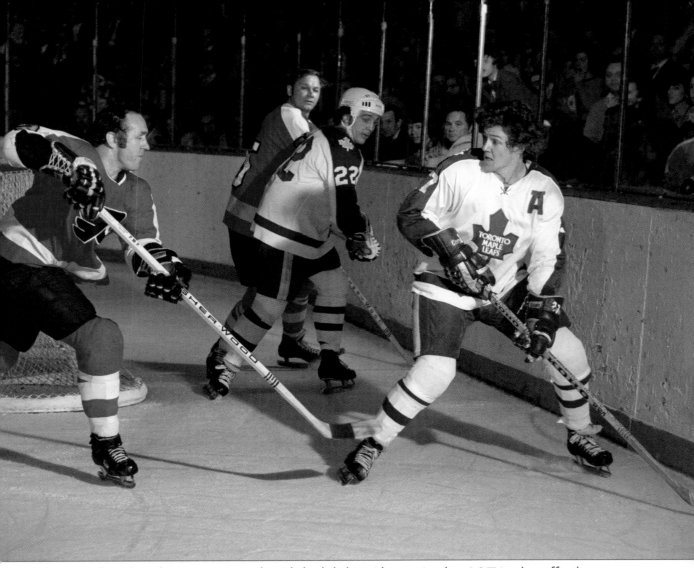

Darryl Sittler skates against the Philadelphia Flyers. In the 1976 playoffs, he used "Pyramid Power" to score five goals in an 8–5 win over them.

That night, there was indeed magic in Sittler's stick. He tied a 32-year-old playoff record by scoring five times in an 8–5 victory. Unfortunately for Toronto, no pyramid could overcome the Flyers. Philadelphia won the hard-fought series in seven games.

Team Spirit

One of the hardest tickets to find in sports is a good seat for a Maple Leafs game. No matter how the team is doing, Toronto fans pack their building for every contest. The list of people waiting for a chance to buy season tickets goes on and on. The team has been selling out games since its new building opened in 1999, even though tickets can be very expensive.

Of course, you don't have to buy a ticket to become part of "Leafs Nation." In fact, you don't even have to live in Canada. You just have to love history, *tradition*, and know your hockey. Or you can subscribe to *Leafs Nation*, the team's official magazine.

Toronto fans are extremely knowledgeable. They appreciate defensive teamwork and unselfish play. The Maple Leafs know this better than anyone. If they don't perform their best, the fans will definitely remind them! Perhaps that is why, in the 60-plus years the NHL has awarded the Art Ross Trophy to the league's highest individual scorer, no Toronto player has ever taken the award home.

Curtis Joseph shows his appreciation for Leafs fans before a 2008–09 game. A similar jersey was handed out to those in attendance that night.

Timeline

The hockey season is played from October through June. That means each season takes place at the end of one year and the beginning of the next. In this timeline, the accomplishments of the Maple Leafs are shown by season.

1921–22
The team wins the Stanley Cup as the St. Pats.

1939–40
The Leafs reach the Stanley Cup Finals for the seventh time in nine seasons.

1917–18
The team plays its first NHL season as the Toronto Arenas.

1924–25
Babe Dye scores 38 goals in 29 games to lead the league.

1931–32
The team plays its first season in Maple Leaf Gardens.

A team photo of the 1931–32 Leafs.

TORONTO MAPLE LEAFS HOCKEY TEAM 1932
WORLD'S CHAMPIONS
WINNERS OF THE STANLEY CUP

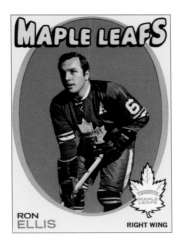

Ron Ellis, a star for Toronto in the 1960s.

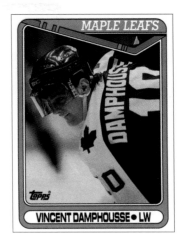

Vincent Damphousse

1964–65
Johnny Bower and Terry Sawchuk share the Vezina Trophy as the NHL's top goalies.

1990–91
Vincent Damphousse is **Most Valuable Player (MVP)** of the All-Star Game.

2002–03
Alexander Mogilny wins the **Lady Byng Trophy**.

1948–49
The team wins its third championship in a row.

1966–67
Toronto wins the Stanley Cup for the fourth time in the 1960s.

2006–07
Mats Sundin becomes the first Swedish player to score 500 NHL goals.

Mats Sundin scores during the 2006–07 season.

Fun Facts

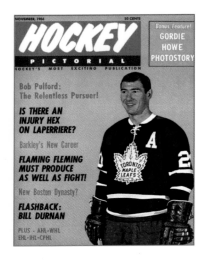

BREAK IT UP, GUYS

For almost 50 years, all NHL rinks had a single penalty box. If players from opposing teams were serving time, they had to sit together. That changed in 1963 after Toronto's Bob Pulford and Montreal's Terry Harper were sent off for fighting. When they continued their bout in the box, the league was convinced to install separate penalty boxes.

SCRATCH TEST

The nickname for goalie Felix Potvin was "Felix the Cat." He showed why in the 1994 playoffs. Potvin made one catlike save after another, stretching with great quickness to stop the puck. The Leafs won three games by a score of 1–0 against the Chicago Blackhawks.

BORN IN THE USA

In 2008, the Maple Leafs hired Brian Burke to run their team. It marked the first time in history that a United States citizen was in charge of hockey for the Leafs.

ABOVE: A magazine cover from 1967 shows Bob Pulford.
RIGHT: A button for Tim Horton's doughnut shops.

BUT CAN HE DUNK?

Tim Horton had a head for hockey—and for business. In the 1960s, he opened a string of donut shops. It grew to have more than 3,000 locations.

FACE JOB

Cuts and stitches are an unfortunate part of pro hockey. Even so, Borje Salming's injury in a 1986 game against the Detroit Red Wings was especially bad. He was cut by a skate and needed more than 200 stitches to repair the gash!

VIEW FROM THE BUNKER

Harold Ballard owned the Maple Leafs from 1972 to 1990. He was one of the most famous characters in Toronto hockey history. Ballard used to watch his team's games from an opening shielded from fans in one end of Maple Leaf Gardens that was nicknamed the "bunker."

THE VOICE OF HOCKEY

From the 1930s to the 1960s, millions of Maple Leafs fans followed the team on the radio. The voice they heard for most of those years belonged to Foster Hewitt, one of hockey's most famous broadcasters. He was the first to say, "He shoots … he scores!"

Talking Hockey

"There have been a lot of great overtime goals in NHL history, but to me Barilko's was one of the best—a perfect ending to a tremendous series."

—Harry Watson, on the shot by Bill Barilko that won the 1951 Stanley Cup

"Put the kids in with a few old pappy guys who still like to win, and the combination is unbeatable."

—Conn Smythe, on the secret to building a Stanley Cup champion

"The Leafs pay me for my work in practices … and I throw in the games for free."

—Turk Broda, on how much he loved to play for Toronto

"Maple Leaf players like Conacher, Primeau, Jackson, Clancy, and Hap Day were our heroes … It was a boyhood dream to play for Toronto."

—Ted Kennedy, on why he signed with the team as a teenager

ABOVE: Conn Smythe   **RIGHT**: Mats Sundin

"With the fans and the Toronto Maple Leafs organization, the way I've been treated here has been awesome."

—*Mats Sundin, on his years with the team*

"If he'd only get angry, no one would top him in this league."

—*King Clancy, on "nice guy" Tim Horton*

"The old players I have are the best. Each one of them has tremendous desire. That's what keeps them in there."

—*Punch Imlach, on his "over-the-hill" 1967 Stanley Cup champs*

"Hockey players are portrayed to be living in a dream world, but it's simply not true. Most of them view themselves as just earning a living like most people—though I suppose they have more fun!"

—*Ian Turnbull, on the life of an NHL player*

For the Record

T he great Maple Leafs teams and players have left their marks on the record books. These are the "best of the best" …

Turk Broda

Eddie Shack

MAPLE LEAFS AWARD WINNERS

HART MEMORIAL TROPHY
MOST VALUABLE PLAYER (MVP)

Babe Pratt	1943–44
Ted Kennedy	1954–55

VEZINA TROPHY
TOP GOALTENDER

Turk Broda	1940–41
Turk Broda	1947–48
Al Rollins	1950–51
Harry Lumley	1953–54
Johnny Bower	1960–61
Terry Sawchuk & Johnny Bower	1964–65

CONN SMYTHE TROPHY
MVP DURING PLAYOFFS

Dave Keon	1966–67

ALL-STAR GAME MVP

Eddie Shack	1962
Frank Mahovlich	1963
Bruce Gamble	1968
Vincent Damphousse	1991

CALDER TROPHY
TOP FIRST-YEAR PLAYER

Syl Apps	1936–37
Gaye Stewart	1942–43
Gus Bodnar	1943–44
Frank McCool	1944–45
Howie Meeker	1946–47
Frank Mahovlich	1957–58
Dave Keon	1960–61
Kent Douglas	1962–63
Brit Selby	1965–66

MAPLE LEAFS ACHIEVEMENTS

ACHIEVEMENT	SEASON
Stanley Cup Champions*	1917–18
Stanley Cup Champions**	1921–22
Stanley Cup Champions	1931–32
Stanley Cup Finalists	1932–33
Stanley Cup Finalists	1934–35
Stanley Cup Finalists	1935–36
Stanley Cup Finalists	1937–38
Stanley Cup Finalists	1938–39
Stanley Cup Finalists	1939–40
Stanley Cup Champions	1941–42
Stanley Cup Champions	1944–45
Stanley Cup Champions	1946–47
Stanley Cup Champions	1947–48
Stanley Cup Champions	1948–49
Stanley Cup Champions	1950–51
Stanley Cup Finalists	1958–59
Stanley Cup Finalists	1959–60
Stanley Cup Champions	1961–62
Stanley Cup Champions	1962–63
Stanley Cup Champions	1963–64
Stanley Cup Champions	1966–67

*As the Arenas.   **As the St. Patricks.*

DAVE KEON
TORONTO FORWARD

TOP: Johnny Bower, the league's top goalie in 1960–61.
ABOVE: Gordie Drillon, a star for the Leafs in the 1940s.
LEFT: Dave Keon, the MVP of the 1967 playoffs.

Pinpoints

T he history of a hockey team is made up of many smaller stories. These stories take place all over the map—not just in the city a team calls "home." Match the pushpins on these maps to the Team Facts and you will begin to see the story of the Maple Leafs unfold!

TEAM FACTS

1 Toronto, Ontario, Canada—*The team has played here since 1917–18.*

2 Ottawa, Ontario, Canada—*Rick Vaive was born here.*

3 Brandon, Manitoba, Canada—*Turk Broda was born here.*

4 Moncton, New Brunswick, Canada—*Gordie Drillon was born here.*

5 Providence, Rhode Island—*Brian Burke was born here.*

6 Detroit, Michigan—*The Leafs won the Stanley Cup here in 1945 and 1948.*

7 Chicago, Illinois—*The Leafs won the Stanley Cup here in 1962.*

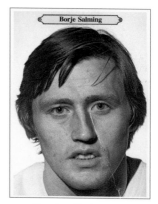

Borje Salming

8 Hanna, Alberta, Canada—*Lanny McDonald was born here.*

9 Delisle, Saskatchewan, Canada—*Max Bentley was born here.*

10 Kiruna, Sweden—*Borje Salming was born here.*

11 Celadna, Czech Republic—*Pavel Kubina was born here.*

12 Russian Federation, Chabarovsk—*Alexander Mogilny was born here.*

Faceoff

Hockey is played between two teams of five skaters and a goalie. Each team has two defensemen and a forward line that includes a left wing, right wing, and center. The goalie's job is to stop the puck from crossing the red goal line. A hockey goal is 6 feet (1.8 meters) wide and 4 feet (1.2 meters) high. The hockey puck is a round disk made of hard rubber. It weighs approximately 6 ounces.

During a game, players work hard for a full "shift." When they get tired, they take a seat on the bench, and a new group jumps off the bench and over the boards to take their place (except for the goalie). Forwards play together in set groups, or "lines," and defensemen do, too.

There are rules that prevent players from injuring or interfering with opponents. However, players are allowed to bump, or "check," each other when they battle for the puck. Because hockey is a fast game played by strong athletes, sometimes checks can be rough!

If a player breaks a rule, a penalty is called by one of two referees. For most penalties, the player must sit in the penalty box for two minutes. This gives the other team a one-skater advantage, or "power play." The team down a skater is said to be "short-handed."

NHL games have three 20-minute periods—60 minutes in all— and the team that scores the most goals is the winner. If the score is tied, the teams play an overtime period. The first team to score during overtime wins. If the game is still tied, it is decided by a shootout—a one-on-one contest between the goalies and the best shooters from the other team. During the Stanley Cup playoffs, no shootouts are held. The teams play until the tie is broken.

Things happen so quickly in hockey that it is easy to overlook set plays. The next time you watch a game, see if you can spot these plays:

PLAY LIST

DEFLECTION—Sometimes a shooter does not try to score a goal. Instead, he aims his shot so that a teammate can touch the puck with his stick and suddenly change its direction. If the goalie is moving to stop the first shot, he may be unable to adjust to the "deflection."

GIVE-AND-GO—When a skater is closely guarded and cannot get an open shot, he sometimes passes to a teammate with the idea of getting a return pass in better position to shoot. The "give-and-go" works when the defender turns to follow the pass and loses track of his man. By the time he recovers, it is too late.

ONE-TIMER—When a player receives a pass, he often has to control the puck and position himself for a shot. This gives the defense a chance to react. Some players are skilled enough to shoot the instant a pass arrives for a "one-timer." A well-aimed one-timer is almost impossible to stop.

PULLING THE GOALIE—Sometimes in the final moments of a game, the team that is behind will try a risky play. To gain an extra skater, the team will pull the goalie out of the game and replace him with a center, wing, or defenseman. This gives the team a better chance to score. It also leaves the goal unprotected and allows the opponent a chance to score an "empty-net goal."

Glossary

HOCKEY WORDS TO KNOW

ALL-STAR GAME—The annual game featuring the NHL's best players. Prior to 1967, the game was played at the beginning of the season between the league champion and an All-Star squad.

ASSISTS—Passes that lead to a goal.

CANADA CUP—A competition between the world's best national hockey teams that began in 1976. Today it is known as the World Cup.

CLUTCH—Performing well under pressure.

DIVISION—A group of teams that play in the same region.

DRAFT CHOICES—Players selected or "drafted" by NHL teams each summer.

EASTERN CONFERENCE FINALS—The series that determines which team from the East will face the best team from the West in the Stanley Cup Finals.

HALL OF FAME—The museum in Toronto, Canada where hockey's greatest players are honored. A player voted into the Hall of Fame is sometimes called a "Hall of Famer."

LADY BYNG TROPHY—The award given each season to the player who shows the best sportsmanship.

MINORS—Leagues below the NHL.

MOST VALUABLE PLAYER (MVP)—The award given to the best player in the All-Star Game.

NATIONAL BASKETBALL ASSOCIATION (NBA)—The professional league that has been operating since 1946–47.

NATIONAL HOCKEY LEAGUE (NHL)—The league that began play in 1917–18 and is still in existence today.

OVERTIME—The extra period played when a game is tied after 60 minutes.

PACIFIC COAST HOCKEY ASSOCIATION (PCHA)—An early pro league with teams on the West Coast of Canada and the United States. The PCHA operated from 1911 to 1924.

PENALTY KILLER—A player who takes the ice when his team is short-handed.

PLAYOFFS—The games played after the season to determine the league champion.

PROFESSIONAL—A player or team that plays a sport for money.

ROLE PLAYERS—Players who have a specific job when they are on the ice.

SHUT OUT—Held an opponent scoreless.

STANDINGS—A daily list of teams, starting with the team with the best record and ending with the team with the worst record.

STANLEY CUP—The championship trophy of North American hockey since 1893, and of the NHL since 1927.

STANLEY CUP FINALS—The series that determines the NHL champion each season. It has been a best-of-seven series since 1939.

TEAM CHEMISTRY—The way players work together on and off the ice. Winning teams usually have good chemistry.

VETERAN—Having great experience.

WORLD HOCKEY ASSOCIATION (WHA)—A rival league to the NHL that played from 1972–73 to 1978–79. When the WHA went out of business, four of its teams joined the NHL.

OTHER WORDS TO KNOW

AGILITY—Quickness and grace.

CENTURY—A period of 100 years.

COMEBACK—The process of catching up from behind, or making up a large deficit.

DECADES—Periods of 10 years; also specific periods, such as the 1950s.

EMBARRASSING—Causing a feeling of dismay.

EMERGED—Developed into.

ERA—A period of time in history.

EXPERIENCED—Having knowledge and skill in a job.

LOGO—A symbol or design that represents a company or team.

MOTIVATE—Inspire to achieve.

OVATION—A long, loud cheer.

REMARKABLE—Unusual or exceptional.

STATISTICIAN—Someone who keeps track of statistics and numbers.

SUPERSTITIOUS—Trusting in magic or luck.

SYMBOL—Something that represents a thought or idea.

SYNTHETIC—Made in a laboratory, not in nature.

TRADITION—A belief or custom that is handed down from generation to generation.

Places to Go

ON THE ROAD

TORONTO MAPLE LEAFS
40 Bay Street
Toronto, Ontario, Canada   M5J 2X2
(416) 815-5700

THE HOCKEY HALL OF FAME
Brookfield Place
30 Yonge Street
Toronto, Ontario, Canada   M5E 1X8
(416) 360-7765

ON THE WEB

THE NATIONAL HOCKEY LEAGUE   www.nhl.com
  • *Learn more about the National Hockey League*

THE TORONTO MAPLE LEAFS   mapleleafs.nhl.com
  • *Learn more about the Maple Leafs*

THE HOCKEY HALL OF FAME   www.hhof.com
  • *Learn more about hockey's greatest players*

ON THE BOOKSHELF

To learn more about the sport of hockey, look for these books at your library or bookstore:

  • MacDonald, James. *Hockey Skills: How to Play Like a Pro*. Berkeley Heights, New Jersey: Enslow Elementary, 2009.

  • Keltie, Thomas. *Inside Hockey! The legends, facts, and feats that made the game*. Toronto, Ontario, Canada: Maple Tree Press, 2008.

  • Romanuk, Paul. *Scholastic Canada Book of Hockey Lists*. Markham, Ontario, Canada: Scholastic Canada, 2007.

Index

The Team

MARK STEWART has written over 200 books for kids—and more than a dozen books on hockey, including a history of the Stanley Cup and an authorized biography of goalie Martin Brodeur. He grew up in New York City during the 1960s rooting for the Rangers and now lives in New Jersey, where he attends Devils games at the new Prudential Center. He especially likes the special all-you-can-eat seating section. Mark comes from a family of writers. His grandfather was Sunday Editor of *The New York Times* and his mother was Articles Editor of *The Ladies' Home Journal* and *McCall's*. Mark has profiled hundreds of athletes over the last 20 years. He has also written several books about New York and New Jersey. Mark is a graduate of Duke University, with a degree in History. He lives with his daughters and wife Sarah overlooking Sandy Hook, New Jersey.

DENIS GIBBONS is a writer and editor with *The Hockey News* and a former newsletter editor of the Toronto-based Society for International Hockey Research (SIHR). He was a contributing writer to the publication *Kings of the Ice: A History of World Hockey* and has worked as chief hockey researcher at five Winter Olympics for the ABC, CBS, and NBC television networks. Denis also has worked as a researcher for the FOX Sports Network during the Stanley Cup playoffs. He resides in Burlington, Ontario, Canada with his wife Chris.

ML   3/12